LEGE~)RE

G000254355

BRADWELL
BOOKS

Published by Bradwell Books

9 Orgreave Close Sheffield S13 9NP
Email: books@bradwellbooks.co.uk

British Library Cataloguing in Publication Data: a catalogue record
for this book is available from the British Library.

1st Edition

ISBN: 9781910551516

Design by: Andrew Caffrey

Typesetting by: Jenks Design

Photograph Credits: iStock and credited individually

Printer: Hobbs - Brunel Road Totton Hampshire SO40 3WX

CONTENTS

Introduction   5

Mystical Glastonbury   7

Heroes and Saints   17

The Fairies   26

Giants and the Devil   33

The Fear of Witchcraft   42

Witches in Folklore   48

Superstitions   54

The Journey through Life   63

Through the seasons   70

Christian and pre-Christian traditions have both left their mark on the folklore-rich town of Glastonbury.
iStock

INTRODUCTION

The folklore and folk tales of the British Isles make for an endlessly fascinating study. A glorious confusion of ancient beliefs has evolved over thousands of years thanks to the many different races that have settled here. In England they have included Stone Age and Bronze Age tribes, the Iron Age Celts, Romans, Angles, Saxons, Norsemen and Normans.

Into this cultural melting pot have been thrown any number of superstitions and half-remembered tales of cultural heroes, some real, some mythical, and many a mixture of both.

Our ancestors lived very different lives to those we enjoy today. Most were tied to the land and had an intimate relationship with the seasons and the natural world. Few had travelled further than their nearest market town, while many had never even strayed that far from the rustic landscape they knew so well.

Nevertheless, their seemingly limited existence was coloured with an awareness of another world, one where supernatural beings lived alongside them just out of sight; where illness or death could be brought about not by microbes but by witchcraft; and where heroes and villains from a past age lived again in dramatic legends told down the generations.

In this book you will be introduced to just a taster of the legends and folklore which enlivened the days and nights of Somerset folk a century or more ago. In its pages you will encounter fairies and goblins, giants and witches, kings, saints and dragon-slayers. You

---

will learn strange superstitions about the wildlife of the county, about the weather and about good and bad omens. You will also be introduced to some of the archaic customs formerly carried out to mark the seasons of the year and the crucial stages in life.

The folklore of Somerset paints the county as a wonderfully magical place.

Witches in Somerset show their allegiance to the Devil. An illustration from *Saducismus Triumphatus*, written by Frome author Joseph Glanvill in the 17th century.

MYSTICAL GLASTONBURY

The little town of Glastonbury has been a place of myth and mystery since at least the 12th century. Today it remains an ideal centre to explore that engaging jumble of alternative beliefs known as 'New Age'. The hippy pilgrimages to Glastonbury in the late 1960s led to the setting up of a music festival on the weekend closest to the summer solstice. The Glastonbury Festival has since become world famous.

But what brought the New Agers here in the first place? The starting point is the legendary king of all the Britons, Arthur. King Arthur, if he existed at all, was possibly a warrior chieftain in the Dark Ages, fighting to keep at bay the invading hordes of Angles, Saxons and Jutes who invaded after the Romans left Britain. Arthur's exploits and those of his knights, his queen and his wizard have been linked to many parts of Britain, in particular the West Country, Wales and southern Scotland. By the Middle Ages, variants of his story were being told across Europe, with many of the most famous romances (as they are known) written in France. King Arthur became an icon of the chivalric ideal, everything that a Christian king should be.

In 1191 the monks at Glastonbury Abbey announced they had discovered within their grounds nothing less than the burial place of King Arthur and his wife Guinevere. They described the finding of an oak coffin containing two skeletons and a lead cross on which was carved the message (in Latin): 'Here lies buried the renowned King Arthur with Guinevere his second wife, in the Isle of Avalon.'

The King Arthur myth had been widely distributed with the publication of a book, *The History of the Kings of Britain,* by Geoffrey of Monmouth, who claimed to have taken as his source an earlier Welsh manuscript. In *The History,* Geoffrey states that after he was grievously wounded during his final battle, Arthur was carried to 'the Isle of Avalon', there to be healed. The author probably did not intend Avalon to be considered an actual location in the mortal world, but rather as a place of enchantment. Nevertheless, in the 12th century Glastonbury and its distinctive Tor (more of which later) could be seen as a fair facsimile of the mythical isle, since in those days it was entirely surrounded by marshes.

The finding of the grave was almost certainly a tall story. This was a time when religious houses attracted pilgrims and generated income through displaying relics, usually of saints. The bones of the celebrated Christian ruler King Arthur were bound to attract both visitors and endowments while heightening Glastonbury Abbey's status, and this is precisely what happened.

The skeletons of the alleged king and queen were laid in a marble tomb within the abbey, although the site of the putative grave mysteriously became lost. The cross has since vanished, too, but when it was examined in the 17th century it was shown to be medieval in date and not a product of the Dark Ages. There is evidence to show that King Henry II instigated the fraud because he wanted to convince the Welsh that their hero was truly dead and would not return, as legend stated, to lead their armies once more. He may also have taken a cut of the profits.

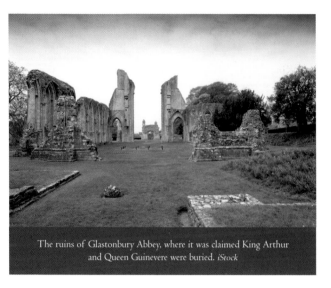

The ruins of Glastonbury Abbey, where it was claimed King Arthur and Queen Guinevere were buried. *iStock*

This was not the first time the monks at Glastonbury had been less than honest in their bid to enhance the abbey's status. In the 1130s, William of Malmesbury – the same scholar who later provided Geoffrey of Monmouth with his source material – wrote an account of the history of the church at Glastonbury, stating that the earliest place of Christian worship may have been founded here as early as AD 180. The Glastonbury monks obtained a copy of this work, but doctored it to suggest that the church had been founded even earlier, about AD 63, by companions of Jesus. These disciples were led, according to the monks, by Joseph of Arimathea, who is thought to have been Jesus's uncle.

In the 15th century this story was further embellished. It was claimed that when Joseph came to Glastonbury, he had in his possession two flasks containing the blood and the sweat of Christ and that these were buried with him. At about the same time reference was made to three thorn bushes growing on Wirral or Wearyall Hill which displayed flower buds on Christmas Day. In time these three hawthorns became the legend of one Holy Thorn, a tree planted by Joseph of Arimathea. It was a cutting of sorts from the Crown of Thorns, and this was why it flowered at Christmas. Another version of the story has Joseph planting his staff in the hillside, after which it miraculously turned into a hawthorn bush. Climbing the steep hill, he had declared to his companions, 'We are weary all', and so it became known as Wearyall (or Wirral) Hill. The original Holy Thorn was chopped down by the Puritans during the Civil War, but a replacement was planted in the same spot in 1951. This was the victim of another attack of vandalism in 2010, when all its branches were hacked off.

The combination of King Arthur and Joseph of Arimathea proved a heady brew for later scholars and fantasists. It was an easy step to turn the two flasks supposedly buried with Joseph into the singular Holy Grail, a chalice in which Christ's blood was collected after the Passion. The Holy Grail features prominently in the medieval Arthurian Romances as the focus of an endless quest to achieve a perfect purity of spirit. Joseph and the Grail had been linked as long ago as the late 12th century in a French poem. Stories – which may actually only date from the 19th century – of Joseph of Arimathea bringing the youthful Jesus to Cornwall became linked to Glastonbury, too.

This history of co-opting old legends in order to make a few quid continued into comparatively recent times in Glastonbury. A long-established tourist attraction is the so-called Chalice Well, a spring of iron-rich water. In fact, the well's original name was Chalcewelle, meaning 'well in the chalk'. But its similarity to the word 'chalice' and the blood-like red tint in its water were simply too reminiscent of the Grail tradition to be ignored. The well was renamed in 1866

Christ's body is taken down from the cross. The bearded man at he back is Joseph of Arimathea. He collected drops of Christ's blood into the chalice he is holding and this ultimately became the most sought-after relic in Christendom – the Holy Grail. *iStock*

and ever since tourists have come to view what they now believe to be a holy well with mystical connections. It's fair to say, though, that the Chalice Well is in a very pleasant spot, surrounded by beautifully maintained gardens, and is well worth a visit. The elegant, Celtic-influenced design on the well cover has been much reproduced.

The final feature to attract lore and legend through the years is Glastonbury Tor. Rising out of the Summerland Meadows to a height of more than 500 feet, this conical hill is a striking and distinctive feature in the landscape, visible for miles around. It would have been even more impressive in past centuries before the marshes which surrounded it were drained. In times of flood, Glastonbury Tor would truly have been an island.

Prominent landscape features, including the tops of distinctive hills, had sacred significance in pre-Christian times. It is no coincidence that the Tor is topped with a church dedicated to St Michael, the warrior angel who cast Satan out of heaven. It was put there to counteract any devilish influences the clergy feared might still have lingered on the hilltop. Only the tower of the medieval church survives. It stands on the site of an earlier wooden church. The head of a stone cross dating from the Saxon period has also been discovered on the summit. There is evidence the Tor was inhabited as long ago as the Iron Age. The series of terraces on the north and south sides of the hill remain an enigma, however. Were they formed through natural weathering, made by medieval farmers or do they have an older, ritual significance? Nobody knows.

We will look at fairy stories from Somerset in more detail in a subsequent chapter but there is one such tale which must be considered here since it has been linked to Glastonbury Tor. A Welsh document dating from the 16th century tells the life of a Celtic missionary called St Collen. Collen is known to have been Welsh but that's about all we do know about him. According to his biographer, the saint had an encounter with Gwyn ap Nudd, the king of the Welsh fairies, at a place called Ynys Wydryn, which translates as 'Island of Glass'. Collen had his hermitage on a mountain at Ynys Wydryn, unaware that Gwyn's court was located on its summit. One day an emissary from the fairy king arrived at his cell and ordered him to present himself. Collen refused. He was summoned twice more, and on the third occasion decided to get it over with. He climbed to the summit, taking with him a flask of holy water.

Collen was led into a sumptuous palace, where Gwyn ap Nudd reclined on a magnificent golden throne. A splendid banquet was under way. Collen was courteously greeted and offered wine in a

The Chalice Well at Glastonbury was linked to the legend of the Holy Grail in the 1860s. *iStock*

golden goblet. He refused the offer. Would he permit himself to be served one of the many dainty dishes spread out before him? He would not.

Growing nettled, Gwyn ap Nudd drew Collen's attention to the splendour in which he lived, comparing it to the holy man's primitive dwelling. He made a particular show of his servants' livery, which were parti-coloured suits of red and blue. Collen snorted derisively: 'Red for hot, blue for cold!' he said, referring to the medieval belief, found for example in Dante's Divine Comedy, that hell was frozen as well as fiery. Then he drew out his flask and splashed around the holy water. In a flash, Gwyn and his court vanished. Collen stood alone on a barren hilltop.

At one time there was a sizeable colony of Welsh people in Somerset, as there was in Cornwall, and it is possible that the Island of Glass refers to Glastonbury Tor. However, there is no historical evidence that St Collen ever came to the county. His presence, on the other hand, is firmly established in North Wales, at Llangollen, where the church is dedicated to him. Similar fairy legends, as well as traditions regarding the Holy Grail, abound in the hills around Llangollen, suggesting that the true setting for this story is there, rather than at Glastonbury. No one knows for sure. Nudd, incidentally, is the Welsh form of the pagan god Nodens (ap Nudd means 'son of Nudd or Nodens').

In 1935 artist Katharine Maltwood claimed to have had a vision in which she saw a 'temple of the stars' laid out in the fields around Glastonbury. She marked out lines connecting landscape features to draw up an interpretation of the signs of the zodiac circling the town. Maltwood further claimed that the 'temple' had originally been laid out by the Sumerians in 2700 BC. Interest in the alleged

The distinctive shape of Glastonbury Tor, crowned by the church tower of St Michael and showing on its sides its mysterious terraces.
iStock

zodiac was revived in the late 1960s when the New Age began to take hold of people's imaginations. However, it was soon shown that many of the signs of the zodiac identified by Katharine Maltwood were drawn up using comparatively modern features such as 18th-century drainage ditches. The 'eye of Capricorn', identified on an aerial photograph, turned out to be a haystack.

The Glastonbury Zodiac is just one more of a series of traditions, genuine or spurious, that have grown up around this one small town. In the 1960s and 1970s, popular books such as *The View Over Atlantis* by John Michell and *Earth Magic* by Francis Hitching continued to enhance Glastonbury's mystical reputation. It has scarcely waned since. This legacy of Arthurian Romance, fairy-lore and New Age beliefs has given Glastonbury a uniquely quirky character with an atmosphere all its own.

HEROES AND SAINTS

We have already seen how closely the legend of King Arthur came to be connected with Glastonbury. From the 16th century onwards Arthur was also linked to another place in Somerset, Cadbury Castle. Cadbury Castle is an Iron Age hill fort probably named after an Anglo-Saxon called Cada. In the 1540s the antiquarian John Leland claimed the encampment was the site of Camelot, Arthur's court. He may have done so because of its proximity to villages called West Camel and Queen Camel, but he also states that the local people 'have herd say that Arture much resorted to Camalat'.

In support of his theory, Leland tells of numerous finds of Roman coins around Cadbury Castle and of the ploughing up of a silver horseshoe. The Elizabethan scholar William Camden later wrote of the hill fort: 'The inhabitants name it King Arthur's palace.'

Nearby is an embankment called Arthur's Causeway, which leads towards Glastonbury, and there is an Arthur's Well on the fort itself. It is uncertain when these features were so named. Later traditions tell of Arthur and his knights – or their phantoms – riding round Cadbury Castle on moonlit nights. Their horses' hooves are said to be shod with silver; a memory, one would imagine, of the finding of a silver horseshoe in Leland's time.

King Arthur is not the only royal hero with a Somerset connection. King Alfred the Great spent a crucial period of his career in the county. The real-life Alfred arguably achieved more in his reign than the mythical Arthur did in his. Alfred saved his kingdom from invaders in the face of almost insurmountable odds and truly justified the epithet 'Great'.

Alfred was King of Wessex in the 9th century and the most powerful ruler in England by the time of his death in 899. His name translates as something like 'Wise Elf' and he was considered a learned and level-headed man. He was also a devout Christian. But, like any good Anglo-Saxon king, when the chips were down he proved himself an able warrior, brave but cautious, with a fine grasp of tactics.

For years Alfred struggled to fend off the Danes, who were invading England with ruthless armies. After numerous defeats he paid them off, but they kept breaking their promises and the battles would begin again. In January 878 the Vikings made a surprise attack on Chippenham in Wiltshire, where Alfred had been staying over the Christmas period. The king and a small band of men managed to make their escape but Chippenham was razed to the ground, the population put to the sword. Alfred and his men made their way to the Somerset Levels and there lay low on Athelney, then an island in the marshes. The future of Anglo-Saxon England was hanging by a thread. If the Danes had discovered Alfred's hiding place, England would be a very different place today.

However, at Easter Alfred emerged from his hiding place and rallied many more men to his side. When he next fought the Danes, the tide turned. Alfred's new army enjoyed a resounding victory. The king then laid siege to Chippenham, starving the remaining Viking force into surrender. Their leader, Guthrum, agreed to be converted to Christianity and Alfred adopted him as his spiritual son. Anglo-Saxon England had been saved in one of the most impressive turnarounds in military history.

A well-known legend of King Alfred's sojourn in Somerset is the 'burning of the cakes'. The worried king had gone out alone from Athelney into the surrounding countryside, spying out the land and

The incognito King Alfred gets a telling off for burning the cakes.
iStock

considering his options. Before he knew it, the light was fading and he decided to take shelter in a peasant's cottage. The poor man and his wife let Alfred stay, but he appeared so exhausted and bedraggled that they did not guess the regal status of their guest.

Next day, the woman of the house asked Alfred to watch over some cakes she was cooking on the griddle, but so absorbed was he in his strategies that he forgot about them and they were burned. The woman was very angry and scolded him for his neglect. Some say she even beat him with a stick. The king was contrite, even amused, by this incident and it reminded him of the importance of always keeping alert. He did not reveal his true identity but left that day to continue the war, which ultimately he won.

Geoffrey of Monmouth, that less than reliable historian of the 12th century, claims that the city of Bath was founded by a King Bladud. Unfortunately, there is no other evidence that such a figure ever existed. Geoffrey certainly paints Bladud as a colourful character, stating that he had magical powers. Bladud constructed a pair of magic wings which flew him high into the sky. His reign ended when for some reason the wings stopped working and Bladud crashed to his death in London. A later tradition has it that Bladud was unfortunate enough as a youth to contract leprosy but noticed that pigs suffering from the same disease that wallowed in the mud surrounding hot springs would emerge with healthy skins. Bladud followed their lead and was also cured. When he became king, he founded a new royal city – the city of Bath – beside the healing waters.

According to tradition, shortly after the Norman Conquest a fierce battle was fought at Norton Camp, an ancient fortress a few miles from Taunton. The blood of all the slain men seeped into the ground and drew out of the depths of the earth a hideous dragon.

After gorging on dead soldiers, the monster began to look for prey further afield and soon became the terror of the neighbourhood. Fortunately, a brave knight, Fulk Fitzwarin, was on hand to tackle the beast. After a terrible struggle, he succeeded in slaying the dragon, and peace was restored. Fulk Fitzwarin features in a number of medieval romances set in other parts of Britain, but his connection to Somerset is shown by the village name Norton Fitzwarren. A representation of the dragon can be seen on a finely carved rood screen in Norton Fitzwarren Church.

An unnamed hero dispatched a similar monster at Churchstanton. The knight tracked the dragon to its lair on land now belonging to Stapley Farm. The resultant scrap was so violent that the lashing of the monster's tail left furrows in the ground and a hollow was created where it died. The field where the fight took place was called Wormstall, 'worm' being an alternative name for a dragon. It's

The ancient baths at Bath, founded according to one tradition by a mythical king called Bladud. *iStock*

possible that the story was invented in order to explain the field's name, however.

An enormous serpent used to emerge from the bogs on Sedgemoor in search of human prey. A courageous villager skewered the creature with a spear nine feet long. The spear used to be kept at Low Ham chapel but has long since gone missing.

Another dragon was killed at Kingston St Mary, but in a novel way. It was an especially fiery brute and enjoyed barbecuing its victims with its flaming breath before devouring them. A villager came up with a simple but effective plan to put an end to this monstrous behaviour. He climbed a hillock overlooking the route usually taken by the beast in search of its prey and waited until it started to crawl along below him. Then he yelled to attract its attention. The dragon looked up and opened its jaws, ready to blast him with its fiery breath. Before it could do so, however, the villager emptied a pail of water into its open mouth. The dragon was so astonished at having its spirits dampened in this way that it continued to gape foolishly at the man on the hill. This brave and quick-thinking fellow then heaved up a boulder lying by his feet and lobbed it down the dragon's throat. The monster choked to death.

A carving on the tower of the church at nearby Bishop's Lydeard shows a dragon with a rock in its mouth, but it's not certain whether the carving inspired the story or whether it was carved to illustrate it. At the parish church at Crowcombe, a double-headed dragon can be seen carved on the end of a medieval bench. This is supposed to show the creature which formerly had its lair in Shervage Wood at the foot of the Quantocks. This dragon was killed through sheer luck. A woodsman sat on the long serpentine monster while it slept, mistaking it for a log. When it awoke and started writhing, the woodsman snatched up his axe and hacked it in two.

At one time, according to legend, Somerset was plagued with dragons.
Fortunately, there always seemed to be someone brave on hand to slay them.
iStock

When St Carantoc came to Somerset from Wales to preach the word of the Lord, he brought with him a splendid altar that had come direct from heaven. Unfortunately, it fell into the sea soon after he arrived. The saint approached King Arthur to ask him for his help in retrieving the altar. Arthur agreed, provided the holy man did something for him first. St Carantoc was sent to pacify a fearsome dragon which lived on Ker Moor, near Carhampton. The monster was huge and savage but the saint was undaunted. Trusting in his faith, he walked calmly up to the snarling beast and placed his stole around its neck. The dragon immediately became as meek as a lamb and the countryside was no more troubled by its predations.

Serpents of a more modest sort feature in the legend of St Keyna. Keyna was said to have been a Welsh princess who had made a vow of chastity and fled to Somerset to avoid an arranged marriage. She sought somewhere to retire from the world where she could devote herself to prayer. To this end she asked the local prince to donate a parcel of land for her use, but he was somewhat unwelcoming. All he was prepared to offer her was a place near present-day Keynsham that was crawling with snakes. So abundant were the venomous reptiles, the land had long been abandoned by both man and beast. The plucky Keyna was undeterred, however. She retired to the shunned land and offered up a prayer. At once all the snakes curled up and turned to stone. The fossil ammonites found thereabouts were pointed out as proof of the story.

St Indract is another obscure saint from before the Norman Conquest. According to William of Malmesbury and other chroniclers he suffered a violent death at Huish Episcopi. Returning from Rome with a party of fellow pilgrims, he was on his way to Glastonbury. A gang of robbers spotted the pilgrims and noticed that the tips of their staves glittered like gold (in fact they were only brass). This led them to assume they were rich and that their saddlebags were bulging with valuables rather than the foodstuffs they actually contained. The footpads waylaid the travellers and brutally murdered them – for very little gain as it turned out – and then threw their bodies into a pit.

A column of light shone down on the murdered pilgrims' bodies for three days and three nights until Ina, King of Wessex, had them removed and buried beside the high altar at Glastonbury Abbey. Indract was considered a martyr and was later canonised. One version of the tale states that the killers were present in the church when the bodies were interred and that they were tormented by devils during the service. They became so deranged that they tore at their own flesh, dying an even more ghastly death than the one they had inflicted on Indract and his friends.

Fossil ammonites found around Keynsham were said to be snakes turned into stone by the prayers of St Keyna. *iStock*

THE FAIRIES

Throughout the British Isles, and further afield, there was for centuries a firm belief in a separate order of beings, human in appearance and customs but usually smaller in size, who regularly visited our world but were not part of it. Generically, they are known as the fairies.

In Somerset they were also known as pixies and by complimentary names such as 'the Fair Folk' or 'the Good Neighbours'. It was considered sensible to always keep on the right side of the fairies: they were usually invisible and you never knew when one might be listening. In his *The Folklore of Somerset*, Kingsley Palmer considers that the county's rural folk may at one time have thought of pixies as inferior, mischievous spirits, and the fairies as more aristocratic.

On Exmoor it was once the custom to put out bowls of bread and milk for the pixies. In the Blackdown area owners of orchards would leave on every tree a few good apples for the fairies. In return, the fairies would ensure a good crop the following year. Sometimes they could be helpful, performing domestic chores around the house or completing harvesting or threshing after dark. But more often they were mischievous.

Typical of their behaviour towards humans was their habit of leading people astray among the hills. Walkers would become suddenly confused by previously well-known landmarks or would awake from a daze to find themselves far out of their way in unfamiliar countryside. Sometimes they would wander for ages, only

British folklore is full of stories about mysterious little beings inhabiting the countryside. In Somerset they were often called pixies. *iStock*

to stumble back to where they started from. This phenomenon was known as being 'pixy-led'. The way to undo the spell, or to prevent it occurring in the first place, was to wear an item of clothing inside-out.

The Blackdown Hills seem to have been one of the fairies' strongholds in Somerset. Here they were described as wearing 'red, blue or green according to the old way of the Country Garb, with high crown'd hats'. From Blagdon comes the following tale of a Fairy Fair, first recorded as long ago as 1684:

'About fifty years ago [i.e. in the 1630s] a person was riding over Blagdon Hill, returning from Taunton to Combe St Nicholas. He saw before him what seemed to be a normal fair, and he took it to be Churchstanton fair that took place during that time of the year. On remembering some story about fairies in that place he decided to ride nearer and take a closer look. However, though he could see well at a distance, at close quarters he could see nothing at all, only he was aware of a pushing crowd. He returned home, finding himself in pain. He became paralysed on one side, and remained so until his death many years later.'

More elaborate versions of this encounter were compiled in the 20th century in which the Fairy Fair is not only visible but almost identical to a human market. In one of these later retellings, the witness buys a cider mug, paying for it with coins and receiving merely a few pebbles as change. He does not anger the fairy stallholder by challenging this, however, and takes the pebbles home along with his purchase. In the morning he finds that the pebbles have turned into solid gold.

The fairies appear to have been rewarding the purchaser for his courtesy. They did not behave as well when they visited our own markets, however. An old woman who had performed a service for the fairies was given the ability to see them at all times. She next saw them at Taunton market and was shocked to see them stealing all manner of goods from the unsuspecting stallholders. She lost no time in telling them what she thought of their dishonesty. But this was a mistake. The fairies 'turned on her like a cloud of angry wasps' and made her blind.

A similar story is told about the market at Minehead, where a woman glimpsed out of the corner of her eye a relative stealing meat from a market stall. She knew that this man had dealings with the fairies but did not realise that he was committing the theft on their behalf. When she accosted him, her relative asked her with which eye she had seen him take the meat. She indicated her right eye. The man blew on it and she was blind in that eye for evermore.

Here, as elsewhere in the UK and Ireland, the fairies were believed to inhabit ancient sites such as hill forts and burial mounds. They are said to have built Cow Castle, a small Iron Age encampment on Exmoor. Here they were seen as dancing bright lights, often in the vicinity of a standing stone near the entrance to the ramparts. The much larger Cadbury Castle, mentioned in the previous chapter, was once inhabited by thousands of fairies, but they fled with the coming of Christianity – the sound of the church bells drove them away. When they departed they left behind a vast treasure house of gold hidden in hollows in the depths of the hill. As evidence for this it has been asserted that the summit has been subsiding over the centuries: at one time the top of the hill could be seen from the village in the valley below but now only the fort's ramparts are visible.

Fairies attending a market. In this old illustration, they are dealing openly with the stallholders, but in Somerset they tended to steal from them. *iStock*

A similar hill fort, Ruborough Camp, was said to cover a subterranean iron castle full of treasure guarded by hideous-looking goblins. The goblins' stronghold was accessible through a pair of iron gates which were only visible on nights of the full moon. A learned man by the name of Dr Farrar is supposed to have located the gates in the 1790s and brought a servant with him to dig down to them. As soon as the servant's spade struck metal, fearsome noises erupted from the earth and the terrified man was grabbed by small but powerful hands which began to drag him under the ground. Dr Farrar had brought a Bible with him as protection and, placing it on his servant's head with one hand, he was able to drag him to safety with the other. Their excavation immediately filled in again, and that was the last time anyone sought the goblins' gates.

Castle Neroche, near Staple Fitzpaine in the south of the county, is a Norman bailey on the site of an earlier hill fort. It too is credited as being hollow and full of fairy gold. When a party of locals attempted to excavate the mound in search of the treasure, they were prevented when one of them, frustrated by long hours of fruitless digging, blasphemed. Instantly, the earth they had removed piled back in, filling up the hole and nearly burying them alive. Similar stories are told about various sites in the Quantocks, too.

Incongruously close to the eyesore of Hinkley Point nuclear power station can be found the Pixies Mound, more properly known as Wick Barrow. Here, according to tradition, a passing labourer heard a small voice crying. He noticed what he took to be a child's toy spade lying broken on the ground. Thinking that its small owner was weeping somewhere out of sight, the kindly man stopped and took the time to mend the broken spade. Then he returned it and called out: 'There 'tis then; never cry no more.'

The next day, he walked that way again and where the spade had lain, he saw a little cake had been left for him. It was delicious. He called out his thanks and continued on his way. Ever afterwards he was a prosperous man, blessed by the fairy whom he had unwittingly helped.

'Toot' is a Somerset dialect word for a hillock or mound, not always prehistoric. There are several Fairy or Fairies' Toots in the county which were believed to have been inhabited by the little people. Strange noises were said to be heard from the Fairy Toot near Butcombe and fairies would dance around it after dark. This sizeable mound was sadly destroyed in the 19th century. Still standing, on a remote hill near Stoney Littleton Farm above Wellow, is an impressive prehistoric long barrow. This too was called the Fairy Toot and believed to be a haunt of the fairies.

A Fairies' Toot stood in the so-called Goblin Combe, south of Brockley. One spring day, centuries ago, a girl out picking primroses became lost in the Combe. After hours of wandering, she sat down in despair on a rock (ever after known as the 'fairy rock') and dropped her flowers. As soon as the blooms hit the stone, a door opened in its side and a fairy came out. The fairy was friendly, apparently pleased by what he took to be a gift of the primroses. He gave the astonished girl in return a ball of solid gold and then showed her the way out of the valley.

After she got home, her remarkable story spread around the country. One greedy individual decided to claim some of the fairy gold for himself. He found his way to the fairy rock and threw down upon it a bunch of primroses he had picked. The door opened again. But his cynical and grasping nature had communicated itself to the occupants. Instead of granting a reward, the angry fairies pulled him inside the rock, and he was never seen again.

The sun sets behind the Blackdown Hills, one of the strongholds of the Somerset fairies. *iStock*

GIANTS AND THE DEVIL

In the previous chapter we saw how some ancient monuments in Somerset were associated with fairies. Many were also associated with giants and others with the Devil.

Some ancient monuments and features in the landscape are so impressive that it was easy for our ancestors to imagine they had been created by giants. The Old Testament makes several references to races of giants and it seemed perfectly reasonable to believe they had once lived in England as well as the Holy Land. Near Bishop's Wood on the Blackdowns, for example, there was a large burial mound, long since destroyed. It was called the Giant's Grave, because it was assumed only a giant could have been buried in such a huge mound.

Not far away are barrows known as Robin Hood's Butts. These were said to have been created by two rival giants who used to throw great lumps of mud at each other across the countryside. The Butts were the result of the heaped-up sods falling short of their target. Another prehistoric mound, Maes Knoll, near Stanton Drew, was said to have been made by a giant scraping a clod of earth off his enormous shovel. Some say the giant was Sir John Hautville, whose great stature both physically and socially has seen him pass into legend. Sir John is also credited with lobbing a massive boulder from Stanton Drew's church tower. It landed near the famous stone circles (see below) and today is known as Hautville's Quoit.

The Avon Gorge near Bristol was also said to be the work of a giant. His name was Gorm. After digging out the mighty gorge,

There are numerous traditions relating to giants in Somerset.
Arthur Rackham

Gorm made an enemy of another giant and tried to escape him by running into the sea. He tripped, fell flat on his face and drowned. The rocky islands known as Brean Down, Flat Holm and Steep Holm are said to be Gorm's bones.

As mentioned above, the Devil is also recalled in the Somerset landscape. There was a Devil's Stone at Culm Davey and another at Staple Fitzpaine. Both appear to have been prehistoric standing stones, although this isn't certain. The Staple Fitzpaine stone is described as being 'composed of hard sandstone of irregular shape, somewhat hollowed out on the sides, partly smoothed and rounded at the top'. It's a squat boulder, about 6 feet high. According to Kingsley Palmer, 'local tradition associates it with evil'. It is said that if it is pricked, it bleeds. To explain its presence, there is a legend that the Devil, standing on Castle Neroche (see the previous chapter), watched with dismay as the villagers at Staple began building a church. He took up a huge boulder and hurled it at the church tower, but it fell short. The marks of his talons as he gripped the stone are still to be seen. The Devil's Stone was removed some time ago to the grounds of Taunton Museum.

A further tradition states that there were once three stones: the Devil's Stone near the village, one on the slope of the hill and a third near the top of the hill. The Devil was supposed to have jumped from one stone to the next. It's possible that they were the remains of a Neolithic stone avenue.

Three large stones near Broadway bear a similar legend to that of the Devil's Stone. They were lobbed by the Devil, one after the other, to destroy the church being built in the village. The place where the church stands now was just beyond the Devil's throw.

A prehistoric standing stone at Churchstanton also had a devilish reputation and was avoided after dark. When a group of girls passed that way one night after a dance, one of them, scoffing at the others' nervousness, boldly addressed the standing stone as it loomed out of the darkness and challenged the Devil to appear. To everyone's horror, something uncanny immediately slipped out from behind the monolith, an animal with a black coat, something like a calf, which bellowed horribly. Of course, it may actually have been a calf, but the girls didn't hang around to find out!

The Avon Gorge was said to have been dug out by a giant called Gorm.
iStock

The best-known legend of this type belongs to the stone circles at Stanton Drew. This celebrated megalithic site consists of three stone circles, an arrangement of three stones known as the Cove, and the single standing stone called Hautville's Quoit, mentioned earlier. At one time the Great Circle – the second largest in England after Avebury — was known as 'The Wedding'. A tale tells of a grand wedding party enjoying a splendid feast followed by dancing. When the celebration was well advanced and everyone was a bit tipsy, a mysterious man in black arrived on the scene. He pulled out a violin and began playing so brilliantly that the wedding party immediately began dancing again. The fiddler played tune after tune, the dancers capering round him in a wide circle.

They did not notice when Saturday turned into Sunday, and they continued dancing to the bewitching music. The man in black — who was, of course, the Devil — laughed with wicked glee, for he had tricked the revellers into breaking the Sabbath, at one time considered a terrible sin. The unfortunate dancers were punished for their ungodliness by being turned into stone.

A woman who was caught by the Devil knitting stockings on a Sunday agreed to pledge her soul to him for a bag of gold. The Sabbath-breaker was called Nancy Camel and she lived in a cave in Ham Woods, Shepton Mallet. Nancy buried the gold in her cave but continued to earn a living knitting stockings every day of the week, including Sunday. When the time came for the Devil to claim her soul, she asked the local vicar what she should do. He told her to give all the money back. Since she hadn't spent any of it, her soul might still be clean. But she couldn't bear to part with all of it and foolishly kept back one gold coin. This was enough to damn her, and the Devil dragged the screaming Nancy away in a black cart.

The Devil was also credited with creating another ancient monument, the Tarr Steps, a primitive clapper bridge over the River Barle in Exmoor. The Tarr Steps consists of a series of supported stone slabs stretching 180 feet across the river. The Evil One is said to have made the bridge in just one night, and he put a spell on it

According to legend, the standing stones at Stanton Drew are dancers petrified by a trick of the Devil. *iStock*

to ensure none but he could use it. When a cat daintily crossed over soon after it was built, the unfortunate animal was torn to pieces. The local holy man was outraged that such a useful structure should be for the sole use of the powers of darkness and he took it upon himself to make it available for everyone. Praying all the while, he began to make his way across the Tarr Steps, and was immediately confronted by the Devil.

'You're a black crow,' sneered the Devil, referring to the priest's clerical garb.

'I'm no blacker than the Devil!' replied the courageous clergyman and he continued on his way over the bridge. By doing so he had exorcised the Tarr Steps of its evil influences and it was now open to all.

The Evil One also visited Keenthorne, according to a tradition recorded by folklorist C.W. Whistler in 1908. At a forge on a crossroads just outside the village, the blacksmith completed his work one evening and regarded it with a considerable feeling of pride. Speaking out loud, he told himself that he was so skilled that 'if the Devil himself' came to his forge he'd not only shoe his horse for him but his own cloven hooves too! This proved a dangerous boast.

One night the smith was working very late on a difficult commission when, on the stroke of midnight, a man dressed all in black rode up to the forge on a huge, black horse. The stranger demanded that his horse be shod. When the smith went to examine the hooves he saw to his horror that the rider had hooves as well. Trying not to show his terror, he told his devilish customer that he needed to fetch his shoeing hammer from his home in the village, and on this pretext ran as fast as his legs could carry him to the parson's house.

The smith told the sleepy parson of the idle boast he had made and its alarming result. The clergyman told him that since he had made a promise to shoe the Devil's horse, he'd better do it, but he counselled him to take no fee for the work. Reluctantly, the smith returned to the forge and the parson followed at a distance, hiding himself behind a hedge to see what would happen. The smith set about his business and soon the black horse was shod. The Devil repeatedly offered him a handsome payment but the smith absolutely refused to take even a penny from him.

Fully aware of the spying parson, the Devil yelled: 'If it wasn't for that blackbird behind the hedge, I'd have made thee take the money!' Then he and his horse vanished in a burst of flame. No doubt if the smith had not had such good advice, he would accidentally have sold his own soul by accepting Satan's bounty.

The Devil is supposed to visit the Wellington Monument every year. The monument was erected on Wellington Hill in tribute to the Iron Duke, who defeated Napoleon at Waterloo. Why the Evil One should wish to honour the Duke of Wellington in this way is a mystery, but it's intriguing that he is thought to do so on St Michael's Day (29 September), for St Michael is the archangel who drove Satan out of heaven.

One last tradition regarding the Devil in Somerset is that he is buried in the county. Apparently, he got caught in the snow one winter and died of the cold. His body was interred under Windwhistle Hill.

The ancient bridge known as the Tarr Steps is said to have been created by the Devil. *iStock*

THE FEAR OF WITCHCRAFT

For many centuries, it was believed that misfortune, illness and even death could be willed upon a person by another skilled in mystic arts or who had been given the power to do so by the Devil. Because witchcraft appears in the Bible (for example, in the story of the Witch of Endor and the conjuring up of a demon for King Solomon), the 'dark arts' were believed in as firmly by educated people as the illiterate.

It might seem the height of foolish ignorance to believe in witchcraft but it should be remembered that, prior to the 18th century, almost nothing was understood about the causes of disease. Microbes were unknown. We believe in the virus giving us a cold even though we have never seen it and our ancestors believed in the existence of witchcraft with the same degree of certainty.

So firm was the belief in witchcraft that someone accused of cursing an animal or human to fall ill or die was treated just the same as if they had poisoned or murdered their victims by more orthodox means. The criminal justice system saw no difference: the end result was all that mattered. By the dawn of the 17th century, however, Europe had fallen into the grip of a 'witch mania', fuelled in part by the resurgence of bubonic plague and by religious insecurity fanned by the Renaissance. No one was safe from an accusation of being a witch. Lonely old women, especially those who had previously been known to provide herbal remedies, harmless love charms and the like, were early targets but even the nobility found themselves accused, often by the unscrupulous as a means of getting them out of the way. Thousands of supposed witches and male sorcerers were hanged or burned alive as the mania swept across Europe.

Incredibly, there is a record as late as 1930 of one Somerset farmer taking another to court whom he believed had bewitched him. The result of the accusation is unknown but it was presumably thrown out.

An important early work on the supernatural, *Saducismus Triumphatus,* was written by a Frome man, Joseph Glanvill. It was published in 1681. From Glanvill we have a number of records of

The witches' sabbat. Images like these helped fuel the fear of witchcraft in past centuries. *iStock*

witchcraft accusations in Somerset, of which the most dramatic was the case of Rich Jones, a 12-year-old Shepton Mallet boy, in 1657.

Rich Jones was approached by a neighbour, Jane Brooks, who begged a piece of bread from him. In return she gave him an apple, then stroked him down his right side, shook his hand and walked away. Soon afterwards the boy felt a severe pain down his right side. After he had eaten half the apple Jane had given him, he began to experience seizures and loss of speech. His family were convinced Rich had been bewitched but he was unable to say who had done it. A number of people were brought into his presence, so that he might point out the guilty party, but as soon as Jane Brooks entered the room, he went blind as well as dumb.

His father had noticed Jane's arrival and, putting two and two together, decided she was responsible. The time-honoured way of robbing a witch of her powers was to draw her blood, and this Mr Jones did by scratching Jane's face. For about a week after this incident, Rich Jones was in good health, but after meeting Jane's sister, Alice Coward, he was stricken again. The boy claimed to have visions of Jane and Alice in their respective homes. He was able to describe what they were doing and the clothes they were wearing. According to Joseph Glanvill, when constables called on the women while Rich was in these states, 'they always found the Boy right in his Descriptions'.

Things became even more dramatic when Rich Jones shrieked out one night that Jane Brooks was in his bedroom. His father and a relative called Gibson rushed in, but could see no one. The boy pointed wildly to the corner of the room, saying she was there, so Gibson struck the air with a knife.

Rich cried out: 'O Father, Coz. Gibson hath cut Jane Brooks's hand and 'tis bloody'. Mr Jones and Cousin Gibson found the constable and the three of them went at once to the Brooks household, where they found Jane bandaging a wounded hand. This was enough evidence for the constable and Jane and Alice were arrested.

If the testimony is to be believed, however, things then became even stranger. Rich Jones began to levitate. He was found dangling from a beam in his bedroom ceiling and on another occasion, while at a neighbour's house, he was seen to rise up from the ground and float

Young Rich Jones is carried through the air above Shepton Mallet in this woodcut from *Saducismus Triumphatus*. *iStock*

over the garden wall. He 'passed in the Air' for about 300 yards before dropping to earth on another neighbour's doorstep. Rich remained unconscious for some time but when he awoke he said that Jane Brooks had taken him by the arm and flown off with him.

Ultimately, Alice was sent to gaol and Jane was executed for witchcraft. As soon as they were behind bars, Rich's seizures ceased and good health returned to him.

Joseph Glanvill reports another trial which indicated there was an active coven in Somerset. Ten women and one man belonged to the coven, which operated in the area of Brewham and Wincanton. They were presided over by a small figure dressed in black whom they called Robin but who was assumed – by the prosecutors, at least, but not necessarily by the defendants – to be the Devil.

The coven members provided lots of details about their initiations and activities. In order to join the coven, they were expected to walk three times backwards round a church. Then the man in black would leave his 'devil's mark' by pricking the fourth finger of their right hands to draw blood. They would meet at night in open places, feasting and dancing, and then punish their enemies by sticking pins into little wax effigies. They also said they would fly to the sabbats by smearing a magic ointment on their wrists and foreheads and then chanting: 'Thout, tout, a tout, tout, throughout and about.'

The accused were fortunate. Changing attitudes to the existence of witchcraft led to the case being dropped despite all their given evidence. However, proof that belief in witches continued into the 18th century is shown by the brutal treatment of an elderly woman at Woodlands, near Frome, in 1731. The woman was 'swam' in a barbarous ritual to determine her guilt. A suspected witch would be thrown into a pond with a rope around her which was held at each end by her accusers. If she floated, it was thought that the Devil was magically preserving her life, but if she sank she was innocent – and might very likely drown. A contemporary report describes what happened at Woodlands:

'Suspicion fell on a decrepit old woman living in the neighbourhood, and although the poor creature was suffering from ague [possibly rheumatism is meant], she was dragged from her cottage, set astride a horse, and carried to a millpond about two miles away, where after stripping off her upper clothes, they tied her legs together, and putting a rope about her waist, threw her into the water, in the presence of two hundred spectators, who cheered and abetted the proceedings.

'It was said that no amount of pushing would keep her under, but that she "swam like a cork", which under the circumstances was only natural, as both ends of the rope were held by some of her tormentors, and the slightest strain would cause her to rise to the surface. When almost dead, they drew her to the bank, poured brandy down her throat, and put her in a stable, throwing some litter over her, where in an hour's time she died.

'Although over forty persons were concerned in this murder, the Coroner at the inquest could not discover the ring-leaders, as no one could be persuaded to accuse his neighbour, so he was only able to charge three with manslaughter.'

WITCHES IN FOLKLORE

Historical accounts reveal a good deal about the superstitions regarding witchcraft in the past, but the lasting legacy of these beliefs are folk tales about individual witches. In common with folk tales from all over the country, the Somerset witches were believed to be able to turn into hares. The reason for the link between witches and hares is unknown but it may reflect a cult association in the time of the Celts. When the warrior queen Boudicca was beginning her uprising against the Romans in AD 60/61, she released a hare and the way it ran determined her plan of attack.

At Stathe, the Black Smock Inn — now converted into a private residence — is said to have got its strange name because of a witch who lived there centuries ago. The local farmers got so fed up with her cursing their livestock that they formed a posse and surrounded her cottage. Unable to escape through the usual exits, the witch went up the chimney. Then the angry men saw her racing away across the fields in the form of a hare. As she made her escape, the soot in the chimney blackened the witch's smock. Despite the drama of the incident, it was after this humdrum detail that the pub was named.

At Porlock in the 1890s lived the Sloley family — two sisters and a brother — who were all credited as having the evil eye. One of the sisters was believed to be able to turn herself into a hare, leading the hounds away from genuine sport and ruining the hunters' day. On one occasion she was very nearly caught, but dodged quickly out of sight; when the hunters caught up, there was Miss Sloley combing her matted hair with a nonchalant air despite being very obviously out of breath. When the other sister was spotted stealing cakes at a village fete, she told the man who exposed her that she had 'marked him down'. He fell ill that same evening and wasted away to an early death.

A Bridgwater resident suspected witchcraft when his pig was struck down with a mysterious illness. His suspicions turned to an elderly woman who kept stopping at his house and asking after his ailing pig in a tone which suggested anything but concern. The woman already had a reputation as a witch. Her neighbours said they often saw a white rabbit scampering up and down the lane outside her home, invariably making for an open window, where they would

A number of Somerset witches were said to be able to turn into hares.
iStock

lose sight of it. They assumed the rabbit was the witch in disguise – a variant on the usual hare.

Egged on by the pig owner, the townsfolk chased the rabbit when it was next spotted, and they trapped it in a walled garden. The pig owner managed to grab the rabbit and he gave the poor thing a severe kick, before it managed to wriggle away and make its escape. The old woman under suspicion took to her bed for three days because she had lost the use of her legs; proof, it was thought, that she and the white rabbit were one and the same. The rabbit was never seen again and the man's pig recovered.

Another common belief about witches is that they had 'familiars', demons in animal form which would do their bidding, carrying out all manner of sinister tasks. They were even believed to 'suckle' these familiars from various parts of their bodies. At the height of the witch mania, any lonely or ill-favoured old woman might find herself targeted as a witch – and many would have owned a pet or two. More often than not these harmless animals would be branded as familiars and their keeping would be used as evidence against their owners.

The folklorist Ruth Tongue was told about a witch at Broomfield who kept familiars in the shape of toads. She would 'send the toads after' anyone who crossed her, as Mrs Tongue's informant explained:

'I knew the carter who worked over to Ivyton Farm and he had to go to Bridgwater with the cart with a load of corn and she [the witch] came to the door and asked him to bring her a couple of sacks of coal back. Well, he forgot and when he come to her cottage she came out for her coals, and she shook her fist at him and said, "I'll set the toads on 'ee."'

From then on, every time the carter passed the woman's home, its load would invariably be upset as the pegs used to secure it mysteriously sprang free. The witch would watch this with great enjoyment, cackling: 'That'll teach 'ee to forget my coals. I'll toad 'ee!'

The storyteller recalled: 'The carter told me he'd tie the pegs down with binder twine but 'twas no use. Every time he got to the cottage the twine broke, and the pegs sprung, and the old witch she'd come to her door, and stand there and cackle.'

This account was collected by Ruth Tongue as recently as the 1950s. It must have had resonances for the writer, for she recalled how as a young girl she knew an old woman who kept 'dozens of toads' and let her play with them.

Once a witch had accepted the responsibility of owning familiars, it was almost impossible to get rid of them again. She would either have to pass them on to a willing relative or destroy them before she would be allowed to die. There is a record of such a scenario once playing out at Chew Stoke. When the local witch became very elderly and racked with pain, she decided she had had enough of life and it was time to die. She asked one of her neighbours to fetch in from the garden a big earthenware pot, which she did. Inside it were a number of toads. The witch pointed to one of them. 'Die!' she commanded and the toad immediately expired. The witch ordered each of the toads in turn to die. As soon as they were all dead, the witch gave up the ghost, too.

The best known of the Somerset witches must be the Witch of Wookey. Wookey Hole Caverns, near Wells, are among the most spectacular in Britain and are a major tourist attraction. Many of the caves' oddly shaped rock formations have been given names after

Many witches in Somerset were said to keep toads as 'familiars'
to do their evil bidding. *iStock*

things they are thought to resemble. The 'witch' is a large stalagmite
in one of the inner chambers. Its resemblance to an old woman had
been noted as long ago as the 15th century but it wasn't until several
hundred years later that 'she' was labelled a witch.

The story told to explain her presence is that when she was a young
woman, her heart had been broken by a faithless lover and she had
retired to Wookey Hole. She retreated into the caves, full of
bitterness and hatred towards mankind, especially young lovers,
whom she couldn't bear to see happy. Down in the darkness she
taught herself the dark arts and learned how to curse anyone she
encountered. She grew older and even more hateful. Eventually, a
young scholar whose girlfriend had been cursed by the witch
determined to take his revenge. He boldly entered her damp, dark
lair, armed with his Bible. The witch retreated further into the cave
and watched as the scholar blessed the stretch of the River Axe
which runs through Wookey Hole. Then, before she had time to
react, he scooped up a handful of the water and sprinkled it over
the hag. She was instantly turned to stone.

An old postcard of the Witch of Wookey, a large stalagmite said to be the petrified remains of a sorceress. *iStock*

In 1912 the skeleton of a woman, over a thousand years old, was found in the cavern and inevitably this too was pronounced to be the remains of the witch. There are persistent stories that the Witch of Wookey now haunts the caves.

Further stories of ghosts can be found in *Somerset and Bristol Ghost Stories* also published by Bradwell Books.

SUPERSTITIONS

Before the second half of the 20th century, our rural ancestors were far closer to the land and much more aware of the changing seasons, nuances in the weather and the flora and fauna around them than most of us today. However, this intimate knowledge was contrasted with a series of superstitions earnestly believed in without having any basis in fact.

There were a number of strange beliefs, for example, about the moon. It was considered unlucky to see the new moon through glass. It was always better to see it for the first time in the open air. The waxing and waning of the moon was thought to affect not only the tides but the growth of all living things. In the days when blood-letting was commonly used by physicians to treat all sorts of ailments, it was believed that blood too had a tide affected by the moon. It was therefore thought best drained at the waxing of the moon to help draw out the badness believed to be in it. A child born under a waning moon would grow up to be less healthy, it was thought, than one born when the moon was waxing. Likewise, animals tended to be slaughtered when the moon was increasing, otherwise the meat might shrink when it was cooked.

The behaviour of birds and animals was taken to have special meaning, in superstitions perhaps dating back to our pagan past. At one time anglers believed that the behaviour of cattle reflected the likelihood or otherwise of catching fish. If the cattle were grazing, angling would be successful because the fish too would be feeding, but if they were lying down, the fish would be skulking away at the bottom of the streams, chewing the cud, so to speak.

Seemingly endless superstitions regarding the weather are to be found in old country lore. This is hardly surprising bearing in mind that the weather affected rural communities so significantly. Some of these beliefs pertained to wildlife. It was said, for example, that to hear a cuckoo stammer foretold coming rain, as did the screeching of a peacock. Rooks massing together while feeding and dogs eating grass were also thought to be an indicator of wet weather. Swallows flying high indicated warm, fine weather, but if they flew low, it would be wet (no doubt this was truly indicated by the position in the atmosphere of the insects on which they were feeding). In regards to trees, it was also believed a wet spring was bound to follow if the leaves on the ash trees emerged before those of the oak. As a popular rhyme had it:

If the ash is out before the oak,
Look out, you'll get a soak.

In winter, if a cat was seen to turn her back on the fire and warm her behind, it was a warning that snow was on its way. A fire burning with a blue flame was also thought to indicate snow. A white hoar frost was supposed to warn of a coming storm. The whiter the frost, the more severe the storm. Some people called the sun's rays when they fell on rivers or ponds 'the sun's water pipes' and believed that the sun was replenishing its water pots with them. As soon as the pots were filled, it would pour them down as rain.

Almost everyone knows the old saw: 'Red sky at night, shepherd's delight; Red sky at morning, shepherd's warning.' Another rhyme gives the same virtue of predicting rain or shine to rainbows:

Rainbow in the morning,
Shepherds take warning;

Rainbow afternoon,
Good weather coming soon;
Rainbow at night,
Shepherd's delight.

It is difficult to know how a rainbow can be seen at night unless
it's round the moon. Possibly the rhyme is referring to late summer's
evenings. A more comprehensive, if even less likely, litany of
rainbow superstitions can be found in the following rhyme:

Rainbow in the south, heavy rain and snow;
Rainbow in the west, little showers and dew;
Rainbow in the east, fair skies and blue;
Rainbow to windward, foul falls the day;
Rainbow to leeward, damp runs away.

It was considered unlucky to point at a rainbow. One superstition
stated that the arm used to point with would become paralysed as
a result. There was a whole host of superstitions in which animals
and birds were supposed to be lucky or unlucky. You will already
be familiar with the rhyme about magpies: 'One for sorrow, two for
joy' etc. It was said that if a crow crossed your path from left to
right, this was a warning of coming misfortune, but if it crossed in
the opposite direction, this was a good omen. A raven flying over a
house or a robin flying into a house were both considered unlucky.
The screech of a barn owl and a dog howling at night were both
bad omens, as was a cock crowing at night, or laying an egg, or a
hen laying unusually small eggs. Bees swarming on a Sunday also
brought bad luck.

Even pretty flowers could be looked on askance. It was a fairly
universal belief that hawthorn (may) blossom would bring bad luck

if it was brought into the house, and some said the same of snowdrops. Even the daffodil, that cheerful bloom which brightens many a home in early spring, had a bad reputation. It was forbidden in any household where chickens, ducks or geese were kept because it was believed the flowers would prevent them laying. Catkins would not only stop hens laying but any livestock giving birth until they were removed.

That so many superstitions pertained to bad luck rather than to good suggests our ancestors generally had a pessimistic outlook. It's a hint perhaps of just how uncertain and brief people's lives were in the past, before modern medicine existed or was freely available.

Our rural ancestors employed a whole range of folk remedies to try and cure themselves of any ailments that might afflict them. No doubt some of these, employing medicinal herbs, were genuinely efficacious, and an old belief that a spider's web wrapped round a cut would help it heal turned out to be true after penicillin was discovered: webs are often full of it. Many other remedies seemed logical but had no basis in modern medicine. Medieval herbalists believed in 'the doctrine of signatures', choosing herbs that vaguely resembled the parts of the body they hoped they'd treat. For example, lungwort, whose leaves resemble lungs, was presumed to be good for respiratory problems. Unfortunately, this optimistic approach rarely proved helpful.

Another commonly held belief was that a person's illness could be transferred to a living animal. For example, a ritual involved placing a live spider inside a walnut shell and then hanging this round the sick person's neck. As the spider died, it was thought, so would the illness. A popular method to remove warts involved rubbing the warts with a snail and then sticking the unfortunate creature on a hawthorn. As the snail rotted away, so would the warts. People

May blossom is one of the cheering sights of early summer but woe betide anyone who brought any into their home. *iStock*

seemed to be particularly bothered by warts in the past and there are numerous 'cures' on record to get rid of them. Another ritual involved laying a bag on a path containing the same number of grains of wheat or of pennies as the person had warts. Anyone foolish enough to pick up the bag would have the warts transferred to them.

Some folk remedies were even more bizarre. Moss found growing on a skull in a graveyard, if dried, ground and taken as snuff, was supposed to cure headaches. A fried mouse in breadcrumbs was given as a meal to children to cure them of wetting the bed. In the hope of taking away the dangerous disease of whooping cough, some people would clip off a lock of the hair of the afflicted child, make a sandwich of it and then feed it to a dog. There was no suggestion that the disease would be transferred to the animal, as in the examples above, but nevertheless this odd custom was believed to at least ease the cough. An even weirder remedy for whooping cough involved the catching of a trout (it had to be caught not bought), cooking it in cider and then cutting off the head. The head was placed inside the sick child's mouth, the fish's jaws outermost, and the child was then instructed to breathe through it!

In addition to these largely unaccountable remedies were charms, in the form of little prayers, which would be uttered by the sufferer or by those trying to help him. A charm for stopping the flow of blood, either after a wound or injury, or perhaps simply in the case of a nosebleed, went:

'In the name of the Father and of the Son and of the Holy Ghost – Christ was born at Bethlehem – dipped in the river Jordan – blessed that river and so it stood. So our Lord Jesus stop this blood.'

This approach was particularly popular for toothache. A typical charm was:

'Peter sat at the gates of Jerusalem. Jesus Christ came by and said, "What ailest thou?" "My teeth and bones do ache full sore." He said, "Thy teeth and bones shall ache no more."'

In some versions Peter was replaced with the name of the sufferer. The charm might also be written out on a piece of paper, folded up and then worn round the neck until the toothache abated. Clearly, these charms had little to do with orthodox Christian theology but must have brought some comfort to the faithful.

Moss scraped from a skull found in a graveyard was one of the more grisly ingredients used in folk medicine. *iStock*

GOOD LUCK

According to our rural ancestors, if you want to ensure good luck then DO:

Carry a piece of coal in your pocket

Carry a piece of iron with a hole in it

Carry a rabbit's foot

Keep a lock of hair from a baby's first haircut

Burn your tea leaves

Salute a solitary magpie

Wish on a falling star

Bow nine times to the new moon

Cut your fingernails on a Thursday

Put on your left sock or stocking first when getting dressed

Pick up a pin if you see one

Pick up a white stone, spit on it and throw it over your head

Take a snail by its horns and throw it backwards over your shoulder

Throw a pinch of salt over your left shoulder

Begin a journey with your right foot first

Look for a four-leaved clover

Look for a double-leaved sprig of ash

Let a black cat cross your path

Nail up a horseshoe, with the points upwards

Cross your fingers if you accidentally do anything unlucky

BAD LUCK

According to our rural ancestors, if you want to avoid bad luck then DON'T:

Walk under a ladder

Put shoes or boots on the table

Shake hands across the table

Spill salt on the table

Sing at the table

Sleep on the table

Place your knife and fork crossways on your plate

Turn your bed on a Sunday

Brush the dust out of the front door

Give gloves as a present

Cut your fingernails on a Monday, Friday or Sunday

Open an umbrella in the house

Bring thyme into the house

Carry anything on your shoulder in the house

Enter a house for the first time through the back door

Throw dead flowers onto the fire

Cut down a flowering tree

Turn back after beginning a journey

Do anything on Friday 13th

Nail up a horseshoe with the points down, so all the luck drains out

THE JOURNEY THROUGH LIFE

Life was more precarious in the past. The lack of understanding as to what caused diseases or the knowledge of how to cure them meant mortality rates were high, especially among children. For the same reason, accidents involving injury were also far more serious. Wars were more frequent, too.

The perilous journey through life had important stages which were celebrated with ritual and accompanied by superstition. There were several strange beliefs regarding the beginning of life. It was said that a child born at midnight would have second sight and that a 'footling', that is one born feet first, would have magical powers. Efforts were made to preserve the caul surrounding the child at birth because it was thought to be possessed with sympathetic magic. Kept safe, it would prevent the person it belonged to ever suffering death by drowning. There are records well into the 20th century of sailors buying cauls in the belief they would keep them safe.

As soon as the mother entered labour, a party would be held at her house called a Merry Meet. The prospective husband would entertain family and neighbours and a 'groaning cheese' and a 'groaning cake' would be carefully cut into exactly the right number of pieces to serve to the guests. Unfortunately, of course, the woman giving birth was unable to enjoy the festivities herself.

With infant mortalities being so high, it was considered essential to christen the new-born baby as soon as possible. An unbaptised child would not go to heaven, but some thought they might become fairies instead. If the baptism was performed at home, the water used to christen the child was often thrown into the fire, to ensure it remained pure and that no evil influence could pollute it. While it was still unbaptised, it was customary to present the baby with an egg — symbolising new life — some salt and, unsafe though it may seem, a box of matches. Salt and fire were considered sure charms against the attentions of evil spirits.

Even after baptism, the infant might be at threat from fairies, who were thought to cast envious eyes at human children. To ward them off, parents might hang over the crib a pair of scissors or tongs, which would dangle in the form of a cross. The cross-shape and the iron in the scissors were sure protection against the 'little people'. If fairies did get their hands on a baby, they would leave in its place a 'changeling', a peevish and ugly fairy child, or a block of wood so enchanted as to resemble the stolen infant. Babies who succumbed to what today we call cot-death were often thought to be the lifeless substitute left behind by kidnapping fairies.

An amusing superstition of the past saw some mothers biting their children's fingernails short rather than cutting them. They believed that if they cut the fingernails, the child would grow up to be a thief. It was also said that a new baby must always be carried upstairs before it goes down, otherwise it would not rise in life. If there were no stairs in the house, the midwife would climb onto a chair with it.

At one time new mothers genuinely feared their children might be stolen by fairies unless they protected them with certain charms before they were baptised. *iStock*

Moving on to young adulthood, there were also some interesting customs surrounding courtship. We tend to assume morals were more conservative in the past, so it may be a surprise to learn that courting couples were often allowed to sleep together undisturbed.

However, this was only with the proviso that the young man kept his clothes on (minus his coat and boots). A variant custom called 'bundling' allowed the couple to share a bed with a bolster between them. Such would have been the disgrace if the young couple abused this trust that few did. Mind you, engagements tended to be shorter in those days.

A young woman hoping to marry into a farming family was often called upon to prove her strength by lifting with one arm the heavy lid of the parish chest in the church. The parish chest contained charitable donations and other valuables and was usually made of thick oak, bound with stout iron. To lift it with just one arm could be quite a feat.

As to the wedding day itself, there was an ancient custom in which the friends of the groom would call at the bride's house with the view of 'abducting' her. Her duty was to hide, so as to avoid this indignity, or better still to sneak to church before they caught her. This was a remnant of a custom known thousands of years ago in which young men would prove their worth by stealing the girl they fancied from under her parents' roof. In more civilised times, no abduction or manhandling of the bride actually took place and the whole thing was done in fun.

A rather unkind superstition related to weddings was that if a woman served as a bridesmaid three times, she would never be married herself. Likewise, a man who acted as best man three times would never wed. But there are even stranger ones on record. If a young woman puts on a man's hat or a young man puts on a woman's hat, they will have to wait three years before they can get married.

If a young person cuts bread obliquely or in uneven slices they will never be married, or will have to wait seven years, or they will end up with an objectionable mother-in-law.

If while sweeping a girl touches the foot of another girl with a broom she will rob that girl of her future husband.

When the bride enters the church, she must never look behind her or she will end up regretting the marriage.

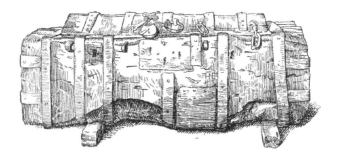

An example of a parish chest, an ancient and massive casket sometimes carved out of one solid piece of oak. Lifting its heavy lid with one arm would be hard work for most men, let alone the young women who were expected to do it. *iStock*

There are equally strange superstitions regarding the really great change in a person's life – death. In the 'Superstitions' chapter several unlucky signs and portents were referred to, such as dogs howling and owls screeching, and these might equally be taken as omens of a coming death. There were many more. Clocks suddenly stopping or chiming thirteen were a bad sign, as were a robin tapping at the window pane, a crow getting into the house or an owl settling on the roof. Mysterious noises such as knocks and raps in the house where someone lay ill were also ominous. Carpenters sometimes claimed they heard sounds in their workshops at night resembling those of a coffin being made. They knew then that one would soon be ordered.

When the last moment had apparently come, people were sometimes 'helped to die' by those looking after them. All the doors and windows in the house were opened wide to allow the soul to escape. At the same time, knots were untied, mirrors covered and the fire – the 'soul of the house' – was put out. 'Passing bells' were traditionally rung nine times to announce a death but their original purpose was to scare away any evil spirits seeking to claim the soul of the departed. A plate of salt, that substance long believed to ward off evil, was placed on the body. No corpse was left with its eyes open for it was said that it would be looking for the next person to die.

After a death, the household would 'keep watch' for at least one night while the corpse lay in the house because it was thought that the soul of the departed might return. Sometimes the assembly would chant: 'It is for the last time, it is the last night', in order to remind the spirt that it had to pass on.

If the master of the house died, it was considered important to inform the bees in the hive of the fact, otherwise they'd all fly away. Any significant tree or bush, even household plants, were at one time draped with black crepe after a death, otherwise it was feared they would wither away.

Once the corpse was conveyed to the burial place, it had to be taken to its grave in the same direction as the sun passes through the sky, that is 'deseal' or 'deosil'. To take it in the opposite direction, 'widdershins', would make the soul vulnerable to malign forces. There was a prejudice about being the first person buried in a new graveyard, because it was said that the Devil had the right to claim the first corpse. Another superstition had it that the spirit of the most recent person to be buried haunted the graveyard, watching over it until another burial took place.

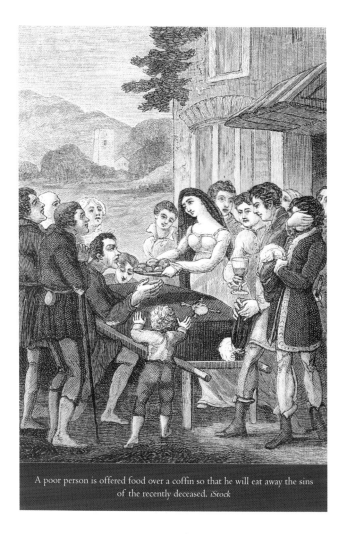

A poor person is offered food over a coffin so that he will eat away the sins of the recently deceased. *iStock*

A decidedly primitive custom, which had all but died out by the end of the 19th century, was that of the 'sin-eater'. The sin-eater was usually a poor member of the parish who was prepared, for a small fee and a meal, to spiritually take on the sins of the person who had just died. This would be achieved by offering the man specially baked cakes, or bread on a dish of salt, the eating of which meant that he would absorb the sins. The food might even be offered over the coffin of the dead; at any rate it would always be eaten in the graveyard. This belief seems to hark back to the time when our most distant ancestors believed they could take on the power and attributes of a deceased person by devouring their body. The sin-eater was therefore a kind of spiritual cannibal.

THROUGH THE SEASONS

The rural calendar was marked by a series of high days and festivals intended to mark crucial times for sowing, reaping and other agricultural activities. These were often of great antiquity, pre-dating the Christian era. Many of them were adopted by the Church, although rededicated and renamed, and have therefore been preserved down the years.

The Celtic New Year was 1 November, when winter began. The coming dark days were defied with a great celebratory feast called Samhain. Bonfires were lit, animals were mated for the following spring and any surplus beasts slaughtered to fatten every one up in advance of the approaching cold. Guy Fawkes Night is a survival of the Samhain bonfire festival, merely put back a few days and given a political context which would have meant nothing to our pagan ancestors.

As a transient period, between the old year and the new, Samhain was considered a time when spirits from the underworld could revisit the earth. It was a time of ghosts and witches. This ancient belief is recalled in our still prevalent Halloween traditions. The Church diffused the apparent menace in this festival by dedicating 1 November to all the saints in heaven. 'Hallows' is an archaic word for 'saints', and Halloween is a contraction of 'All Hallows Eve', that is to say the night before All Hallows or All Saints Day. It was formerly the custom on 1 November to go Souling, roaming the parish in request of small gifts of money to be presented with specially baked dainties called soul cakes.

The next great festival in the Celtic calendar was Imbolc, on 1 February. This marked the beginning of the lambing season and is echoed in the Christian Feast of the Purification of the Virgin Mary, or Candlemas, celebrated the following day. Candlemas was dedicated to new mothers and childbirth.

The start of summer was celebrated on 1 May, in the Celtic festival called Beltane. Given over to fertility and the reawakening of the earth, this was a free-for-all party, with singing, dancing, the lighting of more bonfires and a certain amount of licence. May Day continued the tradition in a diluted form. Dancing round the maypole, a pretty ritual, probably replaced a more ribald ceremony.

The last of the big four Celtic festivals took place on 1 August and was called Lugnasad. This was the harvest festival, when the grain would be gathered in. The Christianised Saxons knew it as

The charming custom of dancing round the maypole had its origin in a pagan fertility festival. *iStock*

halfmaesse, meaning 'loaf-mass', which later became corrupted to Lammas or Lammastide. The first loaves of bread made from the gathered grain were dedicated to God in a more general Festival of the First Fruits.

In between these four seasonal festivals were many others, some of pagan and some of Christian origin, and others, like Easter and Christmas, a blend of the two. Lupercalia, the Roman celebration of youth, took place in the middle of February. In the warmer climes of the east it served as something of a harbinger of spring in which young people were encouraged to choose lovers. It had a reputation for excess that was thoroughly defused by the adoption in its place of the feast honouring the martyrdom of St Valentine, which took place on 14 February. Valentine was a gentleman committed to chastity and it seems his association with romantic love was merely a matter of convenience. Nonetheless, St Valentine's

Day remains one of the most popular traditions in the modern calendar, and people have been exchanging love tokens on this day for centuries.

Although Easter honours the Crucifixion and Resurrection of Christ, there are many secular traditions attached to it which date from pre-Christian times. Eggs are a natural symbol of rebirth and were equally appropriate for both the Resurrection and for spring, the season in which Easter falls. It was once a common pastime on Easter Day for people to roll gaily coloured hard-boiled eggs down hillsides in a jovial race. This was called 'pace-egging'. It has been suggested that the rolling eggs represented the life-giving sun's passage through the sky. It's likely that the name Easter has been borrowed from a pagan goddess of the spring, Eostre. The Easter Bunny may well be a descendant of the hare, an animal associated with the spring and fertility and sacred to the Celts.

'Lifting' was a widespread and peculiar custom carried out at Easter but which has now died out. It took place on Easter Monday and Tuesday. A chair would be garlanded with flowers and people would take it in turns to sit in it while their fellows raised them into the air. It was common for men to lift women on Monday and the other way round on Tuesday. A pleasant performance in the villages, it could be a rowdy affair in towns, where strangers were sometimes bundled into the chair and forced to pay a fee in order to be let down again. Folklorist Christina Hole has this to say about lifting:

'The usual explanation was that it was done in memory of our Lord's rising, but it is more probable that it was a survival of an old agricultural rite. In Central Europe girls leap through decorated hoops, saying "Grow flax, grow" as they do it, and the higher they leap the taller the flax will be. Lifting may have originated in something of the same kind.'

Hard-boiled 'pace eggs', brightly coloured with vegetable dyes, were rolled down hills in an old Easter custom. *iStock*

Other traditions relating to Easter are inarguably Christian, however. On Good Friday, the day of Christ's Crucifixion, we still eat Hot Cross Buns. At one time it was common for all loaves to be marked with a cross. Despite its name, Good Friday's association made it an unlucky one in the minds of our ancestors. It has become a bank holiday because those engaged in dangerous occupations, such as mining and fishing, refused to work on that day. Blacksmiths and those in the building trades would often down tools too because it was considered poor taste to handle nails on that day.

The following two days were quite different in character. Easter Sunday was always given over to worship and Monday was a holiday given over to leisure and sports. Some believed that the sun danced on Easter Day in joyous memory of the Resurrection and it was formerly a custom to rise before dawn in the hope of seeing this phenomenon. It was also traditional to wear new clothes on Easter Day, or at least one item that had never been worn before.

Beating the Bounds was another ritual commonly carried out at this time of the year, usually on Ascension Day (5 May). In the days before maps were freely available, it was important to clearly define parish boundaries and to ensure that nothing had occurred to alter them. Beating the Bounds was sometimes taken rather too literally, however. The villagers, accompanied by a clergyman, would take the young boys of the parish on a tour of the landmarks on its boundary. At each one they would pause and the boys would be whipped to make sure they remembered them. The clergyman would often bless the landmarks, too, especially wells.

The day before the feast of St John the Baptist, or St John's Eve, falls on 23 June. It was also known as Midsummer Eve, even though the summer solstice – the longest day of the year – falls a couple of days before. Once again, this important stage in the year was celebrated with the lighting of bonfires.

There were numerous customs and celebrations associated with the bringing in of the harvest in the autumn. Fairs and sales were held at Michaelmas, on 29 September.

The final great festival of the winter was, of course, Christmas. There is in fact no Biblical reference to the date of Christ's birthday and 25 December was chosen because it coincided with ancient pagan rituals associated with the Winter Solstice, the shortest day of the year, and with the birth dates of rival gods, such as Mithras; 25 December became the Festival of the Unconquered Sun during the reign of the Roman Emperor Aurelius. It made sense for the early Christians to adopt a day already given over to celebration, especially one relating to the sense of hope engendered by the start of longer days and shorter nights.

Many of the old, traditional customs associated with Christmas are of pre-Christian origin. Prince Albert, Queen Victoria's husband,

The strange custom of lifting was popular on Easter Monday and the following Tuesday but has now completely died out. *iStock*

is famously credited with bringing the custom of decorating a fir tree to Britain from his native Germany. In fact, there are records of an evergreen tree lit with candles being set up in a London street as long ago as the 15th century. This seems to have been a Norse tradition, as was the selecting of a Yule log, although the word 'Yule' has an Anglo-Saxon origin.

As we have seen, the lighting of fires was a central element to the ancient Celtic celebrations. Fire gave warmth and light, allowed food to be cooked and represented that great life-bringer, the sun. Fire therefore brought luck and scared away the powers of darkness. The Yule log would be selected with great ceremony and celebration, in much the way we would choose a Christmas tree today. The larger the fireplace, the larger the log chosen to fill it. Lighting the log became traditional on Christmas Eve and, if it was big enough, it might bring warmth throughout Christmas Day and beyond.

Holly became associated with Christmas because it is an evergreen, and mistletoe simply because it was the plant most sacred to our

THE YULE LOG

Cutting and bringing home the Yule log was a major occasion in big houses during the run-up to Christmas. *iStock*

Celtic ancestors. According to a Roman historian, the Druids would only allow mistletoe to be cut with a golden sickle as it was so precious.

The Twelve Days of Christmas, which included our present New Year's Day and Twelfth Night (6 January), were the perfect excuse for having a good time. Where possible, big family gatherings would be held or feasts where the servants as well as the masters would be entertained. Carols would be sung by the poor, and extra pennies collected to help them celebrate later on. A more boisterous variant on carol singing was the traditional wassailing. Wassail is an Old English word meaning 'be of good cheer'. Poor people would walk round the parish singing wassailing songs either for money or, more usually, beer. Those better off might have in their possession a wassail cup, large and often of elaborate design, which they would fill with mulled beer or wine and use to toast each other. Mummers Plays – medieval morality plays – were also performed in many places.

In a custom dating back to Roman times, the roles of master and servant were overturned on one day of the year around Christmas time, with the staff served a feast by their employers. Sometimes a Lord of Misrule might be appointed from among the servants, a kind of fool king. In some military regiments today the officers serve Christmas dinner to their men. A charming custom was to lay the table for two on Christmas Eve to 'welcome Joseph and Mary on Christmas morning'. There was also a superstition that animals were able to talk on Christmas morning and some people, particularly children, would creep to the pens and cowsheds as the sun rose in the hope of catching them doing so.

Finally, it was also traditional to celebrate New Year's Day with a party, reflecting the universal belief that it is lucky to begin anything in good spirits. Of course, this tradition still holds true today.

Mistletoe, an unusual plant that is a parasite on other trees, is now closely associated with Christmas but at one time it was venerated by the Druids.
iStock

More Legends & Folklore books from
Bradwell Books for you to enjoy.

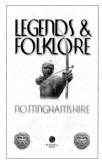

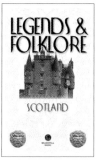

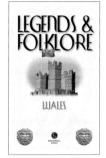

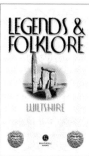

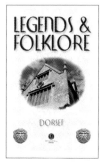

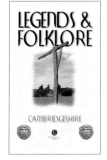

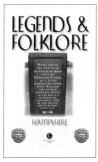

Visit www.bradwellbooks.co.uk for more details